WALKING IN BATH

by
Charles Greenwood

Kingsmead

Kingsmead Press
Rosewell House
Kingsmead Square
Bath

© Charles Greenwood 1978

ISBN 0 906230 50 0

Text set in 10/11 pt Photon Baskerville, printed by photolithography, and bound in Great Britain at The Pitman Press, Bath.

Contents

Walk 1. North Parade Bridge—Ferry Lane Widcombe—Bathwick Hill—American Museum—Sham Castle.   5

Walk 2. Walcot St.—Hedgemead—Morford St.—Julian Rd.   9

Walk 3. Westgate St.—Kingsmead Sq.—Norfolk Crescent—**Royal Victoria Park.**   16

Walk 4. High Street—Paragon—Camden Crescent—Alfred St.   20

Walk 5. Bath Street—Sawclose—Queen Sq.—The Circus—Assembly Rooms.   26

Walk 6. Queen's Parade—Royal Cres.—Lansdown Cres.—Beckford's Tower.   33

Walk 7. Abbey Green—Pierrepont St.—Pulteney Bridge—Sydney Place.   39

Walk 8. Bear Flat—Beechen Cliff—Lyncombe Hill—Prior Park—Widcombe.   46

Walk 9. Kennet & Avon Canal Towpath—Bathampton—Dundas—Monkton Combe—Combe Down—Widcombe.   51

Walk 10. Bathampton—Bathford—Conkwell—Brassknocker Hill—Claverton Down.   56

Walk 11. Weston—Lansdown—Tadwick—Charlcombe.   60

Great Bath with Abbey in background

WALK 1.
North Parade Bridge—Ferry Lane Widcombe—Bathwick Hill—American Museum—Sham Castle

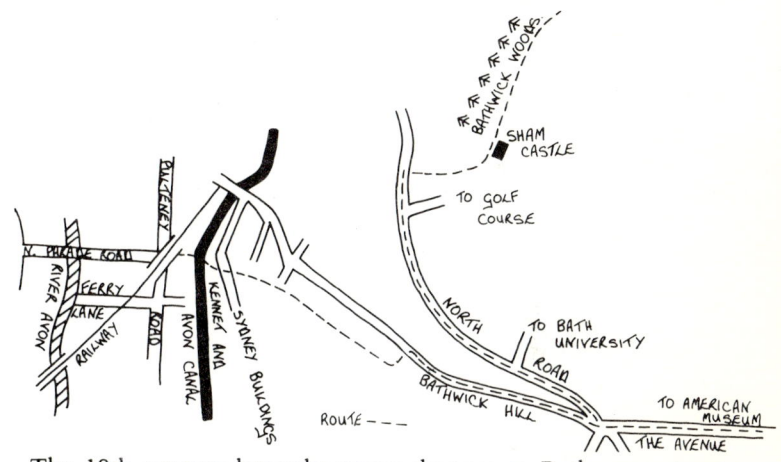

The 19th century brought many changes to Bath, new streets were created, widened or altered. In 1802 Union Street, designed originally by the City Architect Thomas Baldwin, was constructed and this meant the destruction of the famous Bear Inn. Frog Lane became New Bond Street, York Street was created, and the construction of Goodridge's Corridor, but perhaps the greatest expansion was in Bathwick. Thomas Baldwin's grandiose scheme for its dramatic development had come to a sudden halt in 1793 when failure of the Bath City Bank brought bankruptcy to Baldwin and unfortunately coincided with his dismissal as City Architect by the Corporation. The Bathwick estate had been sold earlier by the Earl of Essex (Duke of Kingston) to the Pulteney family, a wealthy clan and a member of the great Whig hierarchy. It was left to William Johnstone of Westerhall in Scotland, who assumed the arms and name of Pulteney, to develop the family estates in Bathwick. The new spirit of Classical architecture stylized so perceptibly by Robert Adam in London was introduced into

Pulteney's Bathwick New Town. This great scheme was never really brought to fruition, Robert Adam found little favour with the pundits occupying the Council Chamber.

Development did go ahead in a modified way, but at the end of the 18th century perhaps the biggest change was the construction of the Kennet & Avon Canal which divided Bathwick in two. It was given considerable support by the new landowner, Lord Darlington (later Duke of Cleveland), who provided in 1815 an open air swimming bath between the river and the canal.

The walk commences from **North Parade,** built by John Wood in 1740 and which was to form part of his ambitious plan to transform the Abbey orchard lands into "The Royal Forum of Bath". Walk to where the terrace joins the North Parade Bridge, and look over the balustrade to the river bank below. Look towards your right and you will notice an elegant little grotto. There is, of course, a romantic piece of nonsense concerning this, and it surrounds the courting of Elizabeth Linley by Richard Sheridan. To understand this courtship and to obtain a closer view of the grotto, it is possible at certain times to reach the river bank by enquiring at the La Pentola restaurant hard by. You will be shown a lively piece of doggerel set in a frame and surrounded with illustrations by the well known Bath artist Samuel Poole who died in 1947. You can see his delicate little water-colours in the corridors of the Pump Room.

Here are Sheridan's lines—

Sheridan Verses to Miss Linley in the Grotto of a Bath Garden.

Uncouth is this moss-covered grotto of stone

And damp is the shade of this dew-dripped tree,

Yet I, this rude grotto with rapture will own

And willow, thy damps are refreshing to me.

For this is the grotto where Laura retired

As late I in secret her confidence sought.

The Linley's lived not far away at No. 1 Orchard Street, later renamed Pierrepont Place. Elizabeth was the daughter of Thomas Linley, and she was to be acclaimed later by royalty and all society for her beauty and brilliant singing.

Return to the bridge and cross to the other side, noting on the left the newly built Sports and Leisure Centre, continue to where North Parade Road joins the **Pulteney Road** and where the railway bridge crosses overhead. Make a brief diversion here and turn right walking towards Widcombe, and to **Ferry Lane** where at its entrance is an attractive terrace of small Regency cottages, called Summerlays Place, and at the far end a cottage has been converted into a "pub" called the Royal Oak. Walk down Ferry Lane, which unfortunately has now lost its rustic appeal, until you reach the river. Across to the other side is the Catholic Church of St. John, built in the late 19th century, and occupying the site which was intended for Wood's grand Royal Forum. Adjoining the church and forming the end of South Parade are railings with a gateway opening on to steps which lead to the river and used in medieval times by the monks from the abbey, and later by 18th century grandees to cross into the pastoral milieu of Bathwick.

On returning to Pulteney Road cross to the other side and walk along to the railway bridge once more, where under the arch you enter a footpath which you follow to the Kennet and Avon Canal. On reaching the towpath turn right and walk towards Top Lock, which has been so carefully restored by the Kennet and Avon Canal Trust. Canals are a world of their own, and it is sad to think of them studded with marinas and boatels, and as snarled up with traffic as any West Country road in the peak holiday season, but this is progress and must be accepted. It has its compensations for where once were decaying old warehouses, cottages, overgrown bridges and leaking lockgates, restoration has changed all that, and once again give the water ways their unique historical backdrop.

As you approach Top Lock note the little gothic lock keeper's cottage which the Trust has restored, and crossing the canal by one of Stothert's elegant iron footbridges you will notice the obvious signs of the care restoration has achieved. The footpath leads to **Sydney Buildings,** and alongside the elevated pavement the path continues in its uphill climb.

Ignore the opening on the left as this will lead into **Darlington Place,** but continue uphill; it does seem that the only life along here is bovine—over on the right are sleepy herds of cattle artistically grouped in the shade of the trees. You will yet again come to another opening on the left leading into Bathwick Hill opposite Cleveland Walk, but continue along the footpath to the final break in the terrace of Victorian houses. Here is a patch of green adjoining Hill Coach House, and a seat where you can rest after the climb and look across to Bath.

This is where you join **Bathwick Hill,** and continue walking uphill to its junction with North Road. At this spot you can make a diversion to the American Museum which is just a mile along the Avenue hard by, and is reached by a short footpath through a plantation. The Museum is housed in the early 19th century Claverton Manor, built to designs by the architect to George IV Sir Jeffry Wyatville. Here in the heart of Bath's delectable countryside is an American Folk Museum, the only one of its type outside the United States. You will see here an imaginative enterprise to reconstruct the American way of life through to the mid-nineteenth century, and so, a once stately home, the scene of that great Americanophile, the late Sir Winston Churchill, first political speech in 1897, now offers to its visitors a vista into the past of early life in America. The highlight of the Museum is the reproduction of George Washington's garden at Mount Vernon, Virginia, a gift to Claverton by the Colonial Dames of America. Return to Bathwick Hill along the Avenue.

If you have decided against the visit to Claverton Manor, the walk now continues down North Road. On passing the entrance to Bath Golf Course you will see a signpost on the left of the lane pointing to steps and a stile leading to **Sham Castle** standing on Bathampton Down. It is worth the climb for on reaching the summit you will have far reaching views across Bath and the Avon valley. Sham Castle is what it is called—a sham—a folly, the countryside of England has many of them. It has been told that Ralph Allen, whilst living in Bath at his town house, considered the hillside of Bathampton Down bleak, and this inspired him to build his whimsy. There is of course a benevolent side to the story. At the beginning of the 18th century unemployment, that evergreen evil, was rampant in Bath, and Ralph Allen a compassionate man decided to build his castle and in doing so gave work to many of Bath's stonemasons.

The footpath from Bathampton Warren is alongside Bathwick Wood, crossing Celtic Fields to join a footpath leading to a point where the Bathampton Lane joins Warminster Road, where you turn left for Bath.

WALK 2.
Walcot Street—Hedgemead— Morford Street—Julian Rd.

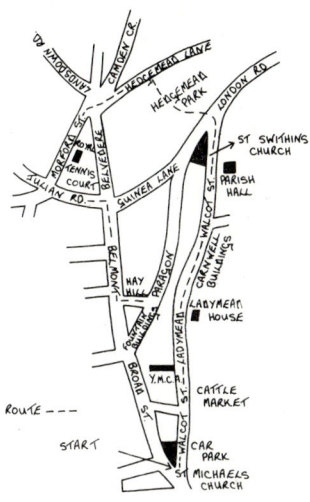

A journey from London to Bath in the mid-eighteenth century was no slight undertaking. The mode of conveyance was by stage-coach or diligence, and you travelled at considerable risk. But the City as of custom old provided for its travellers, that is, if you had the necessary wherewithal, and its inns made a great show of caring for the travel-weary visitor, and to ensure as much daylight travelling as possible in order to avoid attacks by highwaymen or footpads, the departure time was fixed at the early hour of 4 a.m. York House in George Street, designed by John Wood the Younger and opened in 1759 was a favourite venue. Next in importance was the Bear Inn, which has long since disappeared, and of which Anstey, in his "The New Bath Guide" refers to as follows—

"And sure you'll rejoice, my dear mother, to hear
We are safely arrived at the sign of the Bear.

There were other inns, of course, but at the bottom of **Walcot**

Street, opposite St. Michael's church, at one time stood the gabled Pelican Inn, later renamed the Three Cups. It was neither the resort of the wealthy or the fashionable, but its claim to fame was its association with Doctor Samuel Johnson, and his famous circle. Walcot Street at that time was considered a wealthy suburb of Bath, and the situation of the inn enabled its habitués whilst idling their time to observe the "quality" who passed to and fro in their Sedan Chairs.

The Pelican or the Three Cups has passed into history. It was pulled down to make way for the car park, and so another landmark suffered on the altar to the motor car, but the record of the distinguished men and women who gathered there at the behest of the great Johnson, mutual friends such as Quin, Goldsmith, Burke, Sheridan, Foote, Gainsborough, and Reynolds, can never be destroyed.

This walk commences from outside the pseudo gothic church of St. Michael near the site of the old North Gate. The present church is the fourth on the site, and dates from 1835. It is the work of the architect G. P. Manners, and is built in bad taste. Next door to the church is the back entrance to the Saracen's Head, built in 1713, a fine old inn which has claimed many famous people among its devotees, in particular Sir William Edward Parry, Arctic explorer, and a native of Bath, who received his early education at the Bath Grammar School, now King Edward's Grammar School which stands nearly opposite the Inn in **Broad Street.**

There are, of course, stories told of Charles Dickens association with the Saracen's Head, and it has been said that on one occasion when a party of tourists was visiting the Inn, a particularly comfortable looking chair was pointed out as Charles Dickens' favourite seat. On hearing this a member of the party exclaimed "Well, I am going to sit here awhile, and should the great man arrive he can have his favourite seat".

Keeping to the left of Walcot Street—once the route of the Roman Fosse Way—and beyond Saracen Street, a new street constructed to serve the car park hard by, is a group of old shops, and next door to a "by-gone" shop is a flight of steps which leads to a quiet courtyard once known as Gracious Court, after its builder Gracious Stride. It was surrounded by old houses badly needing care, but now most of these have disappeared, and have been replaced by the modern Y.M.C.A. hostel.

Returning to Walcot Street you will see opposite the arches of the old cattle market, and adjoining the disused Corn Exchange. Continue along this side and stop outside Number 66. This is an excellent example of a mid-18th century house, and it still retains many qualities despite the fact that it so badly needs restoring. Further along among the "take-away" food and craft shops you will come to the church house of St.

Saracen's Head.

Michael. Above the doorway is the splendid figure of St. Michael (or perhaps St. George) slaying the dragon.

Cross the road to the other side, and underneath the towering cliff face of the **Paragon** is a disused granite and marble horsetrough and drinking fountain, one of the many in a City where underground springs are in abundance. It is a reminder of a more leisured past, but now obscured by the curtains of time. Retrace your steps back to the other side, and where Walcot Street falls into Ladymead is Ladymead House, the old Female Home and Penitentiary built about 1806 under the direction of the architect James Wilson. This was a reform prison used mainly for prostitutes and at one time its Patron was Prince Leopold of Saxe-Coburg, who later became King of the Belgians. He came to Bath in 1830. Take a look through the gateway, and you will see a quiet courtyard surrounded by the almost classical exterior of the house.

Farther along past **Ladymead House** is the unusual front to 114/116 Walcot Street, known at one time as Carnwell or Cornwell Buildings. It seems that the name refers to the old site of the Carn Well, and history relates that in the time of Edward VI it was known as Walcot's Water and reputed to have prophylactic qualities, and so people came from far and wide to drink the healing waters, the revenues from which came under the patronage of the Priors of Bath Abbey. At the Dissolution, however, the income from the use of the well was given to Bath Grammar School.

For many years Walcot had the blight of the famous or perhaps it is truer to say the infamous tunnel, and a major road scheme hanging over its head, euphemistically referred to as "The Buchanan Plan". The Times called it "a spear thrust in the City's side". The uncertainty has gone and Walcot Street seems to be emerging as a tourist attraction, in fact it has been called the Montmartre of Bath, and the 18th century church of St. Swithins, the only one of its kind remaining in the City, as its Le Sacré-Coeur. Without doubt Walcot is coming back into its own, restoration is taking place, and a little way along from where, you are now is **Chatham Row,** formerly known as Pitt Street. It warms the heart to see the houses here being brought back to life. There are plans to resuscitate the area around the meat storage site, and to improve the buildings at the rear.

Opposite on the other side is the Bell public house, where the devotees of "trad jazz" meet to indulge in their adulation. Further along on this side is a splendid terrace of late Georgian artisan cottages, badly in need of restoration, yet each contains a rare Venetian window which gives a certain quality to this little architectural gem. They were referred to at one time by a former City architect "as slums" and "that they do not meet modern housing requirements, and that if you are going to restore Georgian artisan's houses you will have to find Georgian artisans to live in them".

Close by is the old Mortuary Chapel, and another corner of old Bath which adds to the "off beat" characteristics of Walcot. The chapel is now The Walcot Village Hall and a centre for the Bath Arts Workshop, the creation of an avant-garde group of young people working in an unusual world of the visual arts. In the adjoining churchyard are the mortal remains of Fanny Burney, her husband Count D'Arblay and her son.

Now walk past the many "junk shops", and this is not meant opprobriously, but conveys to the explorer that here can be found the detritus of the past, where browsing can bring its own rewards. At the end of the terrace the **London Road,** the Via Julia of Roman times which ran up from Abonae on the Severn, forms a junction with the Fosse Way. This is an historic site, many Roman remains have been found here, and so it is not surprising that the Walcot Parish church of St. Swithins was built here.

Hard by at the sign of the Hat and Feather is the venue of the Bath Traditional Folk Club. This house at one time brewed its own beer, had an extensive orchard stretching down to the river, and formed part of the estate belonging to the wealthy Skrine family of Warleigh. Cross the London Road to the wooded slopes of Hedgemead, and walk along its terraces to **Hedgemead Lane.** At one time this park was covered with 18th century houses and had two inns, but a landslide at the end of the last century caused considerable destruction, the outcome of which created Hedgemead Park. Hedgemead Lane leads into **Belvedere** where it joins the **Lansdown Road,** and here almost concealed by parasitic houses is Ainslie's Belvedere. A small backwater of 18th century cottages, unpretentious but displaying a certain charm. It is said that Thomas Gainsborough after his initial success in rooms he occupied in Abbey Churchyard moved to Ainslie's Belvedere where the house he once lived in is still called after him. His position as fashionable artist demanded the need of a more commanding residence, and so he eventually moved to Number 17 Circus.

Cross the Lansdown Road to the Belvedere Wine Vaults and walk down **Morford Street**. Stretching up Lansdown from here were the terraces of artisan housing where dwelt in the 18th century and onwards those men whose skills produced the Georgian city which attracted the wealthy, the scholarly, and the dilettanti. Most of this has now disappeared under the Ballance Street Scheme where massive apartment blocks have replaced the pretty artisan terraces which reared upwards from the Julian Road.

Parts of Morford Street have been saved and restored, and on the left as you walk down you will see the 200-year old royal tennis court summarily condemned by the Bath City Council at one time, and is now about to be restored and converted into a museum to house the Bowler Collection of Engineering Machinery purchased by designer Russell Frears in 1969. Miss Georgina Russell is the curator. A former City architect, Dr. H. E. Stutchbury, had claimed, according to Mr Adam Fergusson in his book "The Sack of Bath", that the needs of history would be better served by putting up a plaque on the site.

On reaching the **Julian Road** turn left and continue along to Montpelier, passing Christ Church Hall which has now finished its parochial role and is about to be converted into flats. It started life as a Roman Catholic Chapel, to become later the parish hall of nearby Christ Church during the period when this church was the popular place of worship for fashionable society living in this area.

Joining the Lansdown Road once more you cross to the elevated pavement of Belmont on the other side,—raised pavements are quite a feature of the northern slopes of the city, they illustrate the difficulties those early builders faced in creating levels on the brow of Lansdown Hill. At the end of this unique terrace of late 18th century houses you turn into **Hay**

Bladud Buildings.

Hill, on the left note the entrance to the corner house with the recesses to house at one time a Grecian statue or urn. Walk down the slope to the **Vineyards,** the name given to the raised pavement on this side of the Paragon. It was on this sloping hillside until well into the 18th century that the cultivation of the muscardine grape was successfully carried out, but Bath was growing, and so the Vineyards were replaced by houses. Beyond Hay Hill Baptist Chapel is **Fountain Buildings,** built in 1775 and named after the Great Conduit, "ever flowing with clear rushing water" and which was kept here to supply water to this area of Bath.

Cross to the Royal York Hotel opposite and return to the City Centre along **Broad Street.**

WALK 3.
Westgate Street—Kingsmead Square—Monmouth Street—Norfolk Crescent—Royal Victoria Park

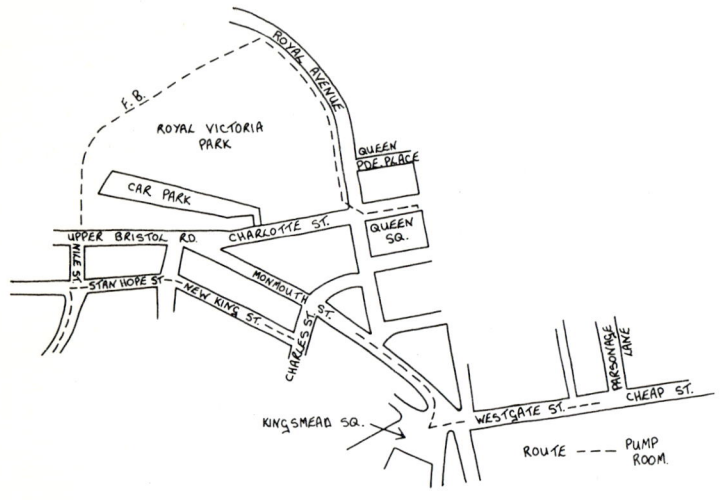

Bath's historic Theatre Royal has recently undergone a badly needed restoration. It was last re-decorated in 1892 when all the fussiness of the Victorians was lavished on its interior. The new scheme was inspired by Stella Clarke, wife of a former chairman of the board of directors, Charles Clarke. The present decor is more in keeping with today's trend in interior design, which seems to please most audiences.

But what of Bath's Theatre history? It goes back into the 17th century, but it was in 1705 when the first theatre was built in the City. It was situated at the top of Parsonage Lane—known at that time as Vicarage Lane—on a site now occupied by the Royal Mineral Water Hospital. The man behind the project was George Trim, a wealthy landowner and a member of the Corporation. The building cost £1300 and was funded by the wealthier citizens of the City.

In 1750 the Orchard Street theatre was opened by John Palmer who had by now purchased all his competitors leaving him in full control of Bath's theatre world. In 1768 he was successful in petitioning Parliament for an Act to enable George III to grant him a patent whereby the Orchard Street theatre became the "Theatre Royal", the first to be called as such outside London.

But at the beginning of the 19th century plans were made for a new and larger theatre on a site adjoining Beaufort Square. In 1805 the new theatre was opened, but had a somewhat chequered career. It gave its greatest performance on a Good Friday in 1862 when the theatre was destroyed by fire. Bath did not remain long without a theatre, a new building was opened in 1863, and this is the one, with minor alterations, which is seen today.

This walk will take you past the Theatre Royal, and commences on the corner of **Westgate Street** where it joins **Cheap Street**. Walk along to the Grapes Inn; you will notice the heavy bolection mouldings forming the architraves around the windows which dates the stonework as being in the first quarter of the 18th century. Inside however the interior would suggest an earlier period, for on the first floor there is a room containing a fine Jacobean ceiling and would appear to be the earliest example of plasterwork surviving in Bath. Three main centre pieces dominate the mouldings in which a double headed eagle and a leopard's head between Tudor roses are spaced alternately. There is a tradition that these escutcheons belong to Charles Granville, second Earl of Bath. He was created Count of the Holy Roman Empire for his services in fighting against the Turks outside Vienna in 1683, and because of this he was allowed to use the Roman Eagle in connection with his coat of arms.

Now walk down Westgate Street and cross over into **Kingsmead Square**. A transformation has taken place here. The terrace on the south side at one time consisted of a tatty row of Georgian houses considered by some as only fit for demolition. This may well have happened, but a local builder decided to purchase the site and in 1975 restoration went ahead under the care and guidance of Bath architects David Brain and Stoller.

So what was once only a tumbling down ruin is again part of the Bath scene, an elegant Georgian building. In the summertime the square takes on a Continental atmosphere with its display of tables and chairs, and brightly coloured umbrellas under the protecting arms of a massive plane tree. The square was the creation in 1727 of John Strahan, a Bristol architect. John Wood who would plainly show his dislike for the work of his professional rivals, was particularly gratuitous in his criticism of Strahan, yet he conceded that Strahan's houses "far exceed the common buildings of any place that I have yet seen"—Walter Ison, The Georgian Buildings of Bath.

On the north side of Kingsmead Square is the opening of **Monmouth Street,** and beyond Tiffany's is St. John's Court, the Garrick Head, and the Theatre Royal. Walk along to 25A–28 Monmouth Street and note the fine work of restoration that the Bath Preservation Trust has carried out. The whole was completed by April 1977. It is thought that this small terrace was the work of John Wood the Elder, and dated between 1730 and 1750.

Cross the road into **Charles Street,** and enter **New King Street.** At No. 19 lived William Herschel, a man of many parts.

Kingsmead Square.

He played the organ in the Octagon (Milsom Street) and conducted the orchestra in the Assembly Rooms. He found time to make monster telescopes with which he chartered the heavens to discover in 1781 a new planet which was first named Georgium Sidus, but later renamed Uranus.

Further along New King Street leads into **Great Stanhope Street** and **Norfolk Crescent.** An area which has been sadly neglected in the past and made worse by the blight of nearby industrial activity, but there are hopes of a better future, even so the Crescent is of architectural interest. It was begun in 1795, and rapidly became fashionable in spite of many set-backs. About this time the Bath City Bank had crashed, and many architects were declared bankrupt. The building of Norfolk Place the original name for the crescent had hardly commenced when it ran into financial difficulties. The land speculator behind the building was one named Richard Bowsher, an attorney, who opened a tontine subscription to fund the completion of the crescent. The architect's name is not recorded, but it has been suggested that it could have been Palmer and the whole scheme was completed by 1830. One feature of Norfolk Crescent which should be noted is the charming stone watch-house of circular design at the north-east corner of the enclosure.

Leave Norfolk Crescent by way of **Nile Street** which leads you to the Upper Bristol Road. Opposite is a footpath which brings you into **Royal Victoria Park,** originally known as Barton Fields or Common Fields, and held by Freemen who were persuaded in 1879 to sell their rights to the Corporation in return for annuities which were paid until 1938 when the last Freemen died. £8000 was raised by subscription supported by Lady Rivers, and under the direction of the City Architect at that time the fine park you see today was laid out.

Barton Fields were first used by the citizens of Bath in 1830, and in that year the Duchess of Kent came to Bath with her daughter Victoria, who on visiting the "Fields" decided then that they should be called the Royal Victoria Park. Seven years later on becoming Queen Victoria, the Park was given gate piers surmounted by open-mouthed lions to mark the occassion. As you leave the Park to join Queen Parade Place to return to the City Centre you will pass through these gate piers.

WALK 4.
High Street—Paragon—Camden Crescent—Alfred Street

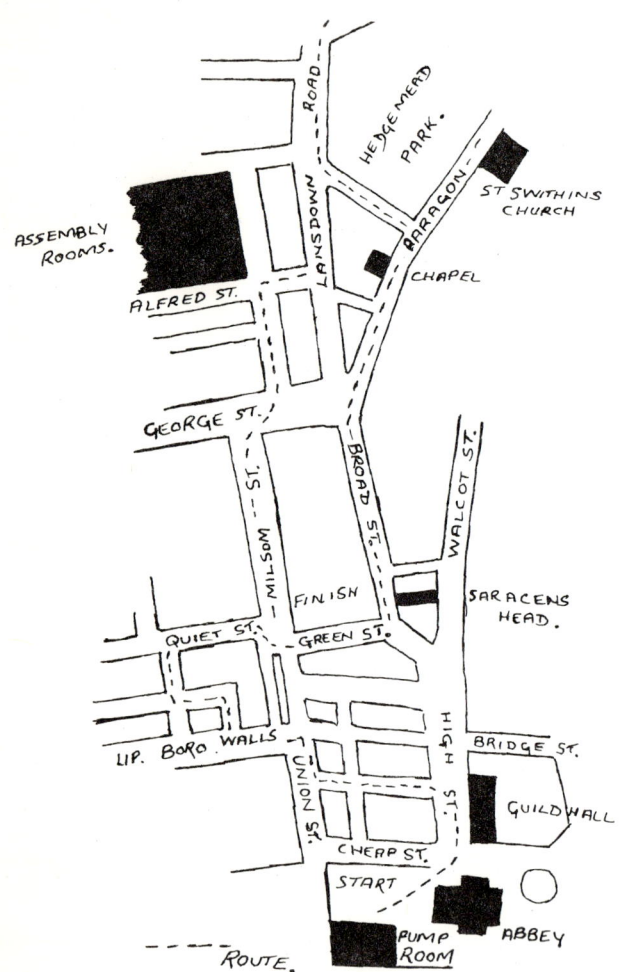

Since the mythical British Prince Bladud first discovered the healing qualities of the Bath waters, some millions of gallons of the stuff which gave this valley its original raison d'etre have come bubbling up out of the rock some several thousand feet below the surface at a temperature of 120 degrees. It replenishes the Great Bath in which Roman exiles escaped temporarily from the austerity of the British climate, and many an old warrior would bathe in the waters and afterwards anoint himself luxuriously with precious ointments to overcome the country's endemic ills. The hot springs were renowned throughout the Roman Empire, and the second century writer Ptolemy refers to Bath as one of the Wonders of the World, yet three centuries later all this creation was buried deep in the mud, for Sul-Minerva was no longer an object of reverence, the Saxons who followed the Romans had accepted Christianity, and the heathen temples fell into ruin.

In the 18th century the Spa once more reached its peak; Queen Anne's visit in 1702 firmly placed the City on the map, when all fashion seemed to come to Bath to enjoy the glamours of the balls, the gambling and poodlefaking under the pretext that their visits were purely prophylactic. So it was in 1705 that the Corporation decided to build a Pump Room, and on a site that housed Bath's first post office and provided John Boyse its postmaster with a door leading into the King's Bath as befitted an important citizen, the shrine of Aesculapius was built enabling "patients" to drink the ritual glass of lukewarm beverage in comfort. This little charade can still be played today, the setting very much the same; the water continues to come, but there have been changes, the present building for example dates from 1791.

Having therefore enjoyed the music supplied by the Pump Room Trio walk outside to Abbey Churchyard and across to the **Abbey** itself, a perfect example of perpendicular architecture. Although this building dates from the late 15th century, a Christian church has stood here for over 1200 years. By the end of the 7th century there was a small Celtic church here dedicated to St. Michael and by about 781 AD there was a Saxon Abbey dedicated to St. Peter standing to the east of the present Abbey and destined in 973 AD to witness the crowning of Edgar, first King of all England. In 1088 William Rufus sold Bath and the Abbey which was by then in ruins for a mere handful of silver to John de Villula of Tours, who was consecrated Bishop of Bath and began to build the Norman Cathedral. The building, typical of French ecclesiastical architecture, was so vast that the present Abbey stands upon the nave only. The Cathedral was damaged by fire and was in ruins by the 15th century when Bishop Oliver King rebuilt the smaller Abbey seen today. It is said that in a dream he heard a voice which said "Let an Olive establish the crown and a King restore the church"—an obvious play on his name. During the reign of Elizabeth I the Abbey had again fallen on bad times and after visiting the City the Queen ordered a nationwide collection for the restoration of the Abbey.

Leave Abbey Churchyard by way of Wade's Passage in the North East corner, and in passing note the large Palladian house on your left built about 1720, and once occupied by General Wade, Scotland's early road builder. Cross the High Street to the **Guildhall** and enquire from the attendant if the Banqueting Room is open to viewing. It is of course a beautiful room and on no account should it be missed, but first a little information about the building. The first Guildhall cost a mere £194 to build, that was in 1569, the second was built in 1625 following a visit by Inigo Jones, and this served the city for 150 years until the present Guildhall was completed in 1778 and immediately recognised as a masterpiece. Thomas Atwood, the City architect of the time, commenced the building but died in 1775 leaving his assistant Thomas Baldwin to complete. The Banqueting Room, perhaps the city's finest Georgian interior, conforms to the popular Robert Adam style, note the Corinthian capitals, the frieze with its garlands and gilded rams head and of course the musicians gallery, note also the fine chandeliers which were supplied in 1778 by William Parker of Whitefriars London. In the late 18th century this beautiful room became the rendezvous of all the wits and beauties of the fashionable life of Bath.

Now return to the High Street and cross to Northumberland Place opposite, a narrow entry leads into this picturesque court of colourful small shops, and temporarily your tour of Bath will be forgotten. However **Union Street** is reached and you cross to the large handsome stone building towards your right, the Royal Mineral Water Hospital, standing on the corner of **Upper Borough Walls.** Beau Nash, Ralph Allen, and John Wood Senior are the names most commonly associated in the public mind with the founding of this charity. Under the first flush of emotion caused by a sermon on Christian charity which was heard in the Abbey this trio endeavoured to enlist support for a scheme to provide a hospital for the deserving poor who came to Bath for their health. Work began in 1738 and the first stone was laid at the north east corner of the building by William Pulteney. In 1793 the architect John Palmer was employed to add the attic storey, spoiling completely John Wood's original design. The adjoining buildings were added in 1850, but note the relief of the "Good Samaritan" in the pediment over the main front.

Opposite the hospital is a fragment of the old Saxon Wall, all that remains of the Saxon town that grew up on the carcase of the once flourishing Roman Spa. Now enter the cobbled alleyway to the right of the wall and walk on into **Trim Street,** named after the landowner George Trim. Building of Trim Street commenced in 1707, thus being one of the earliest streets to be built outside the City Walls. George Trim, a wealthy clothier and a member of Bath Corporation, met serious opposition in trying to extend the City, but he defied his critics and proceeded. New building and the use of existing houses as workshops has completely changed the character of this once fashionable street. No. 5 appears to be unscathed with the passage of time, built in 1730 it still retains a well preserved facade and an arms trophy in the doorway pediment. The house belonged to General Wolfe's mother and the hero of Quebec (1759) stayed here on many occasions when he was not fighting the French.

The entry under St. John's Gate or Trim Bridge leads into **Queen Street** with its shops of antique character carefully retained by the owners who have wisely discovered it to be the hen which lays their golden eggs, and so into **Quiet Street** and here turn right. At No. 9 was the "The Auction Mart and Bazaar" built in 1824 by Henry Goodridge; do note the fine segmental arch to the window, and the figures in the niches on either side representing "Commerce" and "Genius". Opposite at No. 6 stood Hammermeister's renowned Havana Cigar Shop and around the corner where Milsom Street melts into Old Bond Street stood Madame Meyer's Café Bernina with its whirring cuckoo clock: now, sadly, both have gone.

Cross to **Green Street** which takes its name from the Bowling Green which existed close by and continue down to **Broad Street.** Over to the right is the Saracens Head built at the beginning of the 18th century, although its gabled elevation would indicate an earlier date. Charles Dickens stayed here and is supposed to have written part of his Pickwick Papers, and to have met a certain old coach driver by the name of Weller here. Opposite at No. 7 is the shop of James Payne & Son, anatomical shoemakers, where it is still possible to see an Elizabethan house, the home in 1593 of Sir Richard Button, and which stands at the rear of the present premises. Further along on the same side is the Grammar School of King Edward VI built in 1752. At the top of Broad Street you cross to the raised pavement on the far right still known as the **Vineyards,** and up to 1759 when building leases were granted, a vineyard existed on this spot. Walk past some early 18th century cottages to the Countess of Huntingdon's Chapel, opened in 1765. Selina, Lady Huntingdon, who bought the chapel was born in 1707, converted to Methodism by her sister in law Lady Margaret Hastings, and married the Earl of Huntingdon in 1728, and died in 1791. From this chapel the Countess directed her efforts to encourage the aristocracy and fashionable world to absorb the spirit of Wesley and Whitefield who preached here often.

Facing the Vineyards you will notice an archway with steps which lead down from the Paragon—built by Atwood in 1771—to the Old Ladymead district of Walcot, the iron pillars and handrail were added in 1817. From the Vineyards looking east you will observe the elegant curve of the **Paragon,** but walk to the far end: at No. 33 Sarah Siddons lived, and further along is the parish church of St. Swithin's, Walcot. The population of Walcot had increased considerably by the mid-18th century, and so it was necessary to rebuild the church employing John Palmer as the architect. The new church was opened in 1780 and the church and spire finished by 1790. The interior, whilst lacking in originality, displays excellent craftsmanship in a restrained style. The architect is buried here and the parish register commemorates the marriage of Jane Austen's parents, and also records the burial in the church of her father. Here also rests Fanny Burney, novelist and diarist, lifelong friend of Doctor Samuel Johnson.

Cross the London Road to **Hedgemead Park,** created as a result of a landslip, and turn west to climb Guinea Lane, a shabby little back street which has seen better days, to Lansdown Road and turn right to walk along the Belvedere leading into Camden Crescent, or as originally called Upper Camden Place. The Crescent commemorates Charles Pratt, Earl Camden, Lord Chancellor (1766–70), and Recorder for Bath, and was planned to consist of 32 houses. Building began in 1788 to the design of the architect John Eveleigh; there were difficulties with ground levels, and a landslip at the far end curtailed further development, but even today in its truncated form the Crescent creates an impressive prospect from most viewpoints in Bath.

Returning to the Lansdown Road cross to the entrance to **Alfred Street** built by Wood in 1768. In 1782 at No. 2 settled the Lawrence family, the young son Thomas had already earned a reputation as a portrait painter, and it was on his income as a painter that the family were able to live in this fashionable part of the City so near the Assembly Rooms. Thomas later in life was knighted by the Prince Regent and made President of the Royal Academy. Bartlett Street on the south side of Alfred Street leads to George Street and back to the city centre.

WALK 5.
Bath Street—Sawclose—Queen Square—The Circus—Assembly Rooms

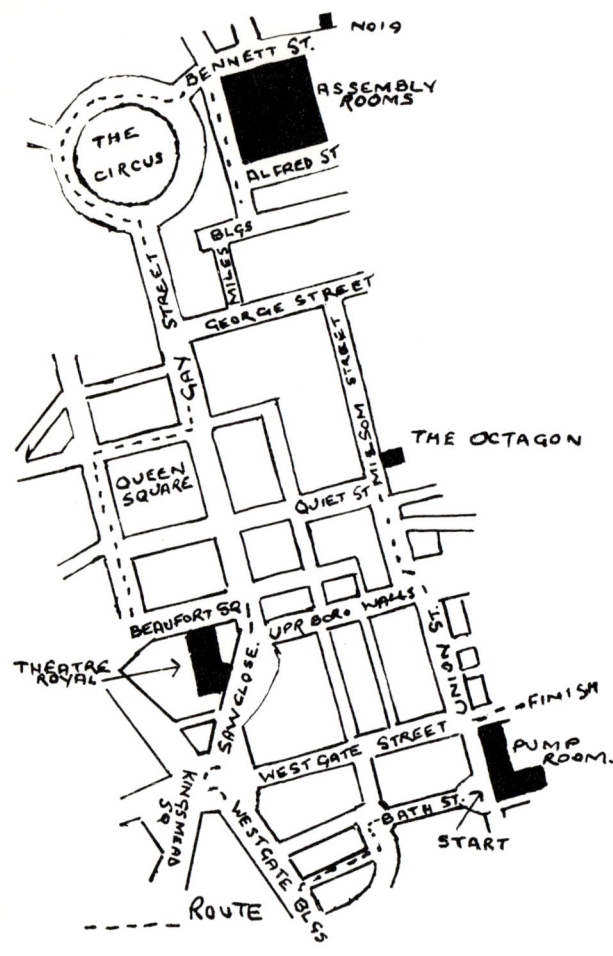

The most outstanding feature about Bath is that it became a city of one period, within 100 years from a medieval town confined strictly within its Saxon walls with a population of less than 3000, it developed into a beautiful Georgian city of some 30,000 inhabitants. Under the rule of a Welshman from Swansea, Richard "Beau" Nash, during the first half of the 18th century, Bath acquired an unrivalled eminence, but there was much Royal patronage during the late 17th century, yet Samuel Pepys on visiting the city in 1668 referred to it as a dirty unkempt place much frequented by cardsharps, pickpockets, and quack doctors. Yet the worthy visitors came and Nash saw the advantages to be obtained by combining entertainment with "taking the waters", and as Master of Ceremonies he set himself the task of cleaning up the town, and became a force in civilising the rough and earthy manners of Georgian society. Each year that passed brought the city more visitors and increased prosperity, and Nash's influence kept pace with the resort's progress. He has recently been described "as an impudent arrogant pleb who achieved the reforms that he did through pure force of personality".

On this walk you will see the two houses occupied by Nash during his lifetime in Bath. The first mansion was in **St John's Court,** and when it was first purchased by Nash it was considered the most imposing residence in Bath, and the second a much smaller house where the now ageing Nash deprived of much of his income from the gaming houses was forced to move to is only a few yards away.

The Bath Improvement Act of 1789 was to effect some necessary clearance in the older city and to improve the approaches to the baths. **Bath Street** came within that order providing covered access between the King's Bath and the Cross and Hot Baths consisting of two colonnades of plain Ionic columns, a most pleasing design created by Thomas Baldwin, the City architect at that time. Bath Street makes an interesting start to this walk, and so commencing from the fountain at the Pump Room end walk down to the Cross Bath, the only bath in which a casual visitor can splash about in the 18th century manner. It derived its name from a cross erected in the centre to commemorate the satisfaction of Mary of Modena, wife of

James II, "on having bathed well", when the bath was redesigned in 1784 the cross was removed. On the otherside of Hot Bath Street is the Royal Hot Bath, built about 1778 and the only civic building John Wood the Younger was directly commissioned to design.

To the rear of the Cross Bath is the Hospital of St. John the Baptist, a charity founded way back in 1180 by Bishop Reginald of Bath. Passing through the fine entrance formed by an arched opening consisting of Doric columns and pediment you enter the quiet courtyard of Chapel Court. The buildings forming the north and east sides together with the adjacent Chandos Buildings were John Wood the Elder's first considerable work in Bath, dating from 1727. Under the patronage of the wealthy Duke of Chandos the scheme of rebuilding went ahead and the hospital received a new lease of life. The almshouse chapel on the left as you enter is the work of the architect William Killigrew and was completed in 1723. Note too how the rebuilding plan blends sympathetically with Wood's earlier building.

A gateway leads into **Westgate Buildings** and here you turn right, but before doing so take a look at Abbey Church House on the left. Formerly known as Hetling House it was built in 1572 by Sir Walter Hungerford and was frequently visited by royalty. Follow the street to where it falls into Kingsmead Square over which a great plane tree spreads its arms, and allow your eyes to travel to the west side and to the almost baroque front of Rosewell House. It formed part of a group built in 1736 by Thomas Rosewell from designs by Strahan, the Bristol architect, and which may account for the strong German–Flemish influence in design common with certain buildings in Bristol.

Hard by is **Sawclose** and the Theatre Royal built by John Palmer to replace the Orchard Street theatre. In 1805 the first theatre was opened and partially destroyed by fire in 1862. It was rebuilt immediately which meant saving the fine elevation facing Beaufort Square, and opened again in 1863. **St. John's Court** is on the left of the theatre and the first house one of a group of four built by Thomas Greenway in 1720 was Beau Nash's town house. It would have been an impressive mansion, the most imposing in Bath, and when Nash moved in, an assortment of the finest furniture of the age accompanied him. The main reception rooms gleamed with an extravagant decor of crystal and gold. Richard "Beau" Nash was the son of an unsuccessful Swansea glass blower and with his fortunes at low ebb he arrived in Bath in 1705. He was a compulsive gambler and womanizer, and it was not long before he had the gaming establishments well and truly tied up, and a mistress installed at St. John's Court. The tongues of scandal wagged, and on one occasion Nash was branded as a "whoremonger" by a coffee house gossip, he was furious and confronted his accuser and demanded an explanation. "I've been informed it is true"; "Then" replied Nash, "you are misinformed, I acknowledge I have a woman living in my house, but if I do keep her a man can no more be termed a whoremonger for having one whore in the house than a cheesemonger for having one cheese".

Unfortunately it is difficult to see this fine house as it might have been, because part of it has been gutted to take the entrance and the staircase of the adjoining theatre and to add further to this execrable addition the Garrick's Head occupies the rear. On the right as you face the theatre entrance is Beau Nash's second house, now a restaurant. Changes in the gaming laws in 1745, and an unsuccessful court action led to Nash's financial downfall and he was compelled to move to this smaller establishment, and it was here that Nash, whose influence had so changed Bath, died, embittered and impoverished. The house is another fine example of Greenway's building, but do note over the fine entrance the curious carved eagles perched on their pedestals.

Further along Barton Street is the entrance to Beaufort Square, still a quiet and retired backwater, and around which is the original front to the Theatre Royal by George Dance, and a terrace of charming little houses built by Strahan in 1730. At the far end of the square you turn right into Prince's Street, named after Frederick Prince of Wales, and a short walk leads into **Queen Square,** John Wood's great undertaking beyond the city walls. Commenced in 1729, the last house was finished in 1736. At No. 13 lived for a short time Jane Austen and here much of her work on "Northanger Abbey" was completed.

Cross to the North side and admire Wood's treatment of this splendid terrace—he was reputed to have lived at No. 24. The square was the most fashionable residential quarter in the city, aided no doubt by Frederick Prince of Wales who, having quarrelled with his father George II in 1737, came to Bath in 1738 and lived here for a time. The obelisk in the centre of the lawn with an inscription by Alexander Pope was erected by Beau Nash to commemorate this visit.

The Circus.

John Wood's original layout for the gardens consisted of parterres surrounded by a low balustraded wall which was entered through the middle of each side by means of iron gates set between stone piers. The gardens as such disappeared a long time ago, and the stone wall replaced by railings, which were removed during the Second World War. However as a result of the endeavours of the Bath Preservation Trust the railings have been restored and were officially handed over to the City on December 10th 1977.

Walk along to the north east corner of the square and to the entrance of **Gay Street;** on the further side at No. 41 lived John

Wood's equally accomplished son John Wood the Younger. Through a ground floor window it is possible to see a small tiled room, an 18th century ladies powder room. Gay Street leads into **The Circus,** perhaps the finest tribute to the genius of Wood Senior. Originally it was to be called King's Circus and it is interesting to note that in 1753 Wood entered into an indenture with William Pitt, later Earl of Chatham, to build a house, now 7 and 8 the Circus. Wood did not live to see the completion of his masterpiece for on May 23 1754 he died, leaving his work to be finished by his son. Almost every other house is famous as the abode of some celebrated visitor or resident. Thomas Gainsborough lived at No. 17 and Lord Clive of India lived at No. 14 during the months that preceded his death in 1774. Dr. Livingstone stayed for a short time at No. 13 while on a brief visit to England after his discovery of the Zambesi River, to name just a few.

Bennett Street opens out from the Circus, and on the right are the **Assembly Rooms** or the Upper Rooms of John Wood the Younger. However walk a little further along to No. 19. Towards the end of the 18th century it was commonplace for half-pay officers, retired naval men, and prosperous clothiers to retire to Bath where they found living cheaper than London, and so it is not surprising that Admiral Arthur Phillip, late Governor of New South Wales and founder of Australia after a distinguished naval career, retired to Bath in 1806 and bought No. 19 Bennett Street to mix with such characters as Capt. Wentworth, Admiral Croft, and the Elliot family, who so convincingly come alive under the skilful pen of Jane Austen in the novel "Persuasion". Phillip died in 1814 and is buried in the Parish Church at Bathampton (see the walk to Bathampton).

Return to the **Assembly Rooms,** built in 1771 to satisfy the needs of fashionable Bath which by then had moved away from the centre to the terraces on Lansdown Hill. Robert Adam was first invited to submit a scheme for a "suite of rooms to be erected on a site east of the Circus". It was far too costly to even be considered, and John Wood's less ambitious plan was accepted costing only £20,000. The exterior is a perfectly unpretentious building and belies the splendid suite of rooms within. They became the centre of Bath's social life in the late

18th century and many famous people performed here—Franz Liszt, Johann Strauss the Elder and Dickens gave his celebrated readings here. The Rooms belong to the National Trust, and are open to the public together with the famous Museum of Costume.

Alfred Street is on the far side of the forecourt, and in passing the end of this cul-de-sac note the house with the bust of King Alfred over the doorway and the fine old ironwork in front showing the extinguishers employed to put out the flambeaux which the footmen used to carry lighted at the rear of the carriages during a night drive through the streets. Ahead is the opening to Miles Buildings, another of the many unknown backwaters of Bath, and on reaching a passage turn right, passing a pretty terrace of Georgian cottages leading to a raised pavement, now turn left and walk past the Hole in the Wall restaurant to the top of Milsom Street crossing George Street to enter this worthy thoroughfare, a shopping street of dignity. At the far end of Milsom Street is Somersetshire Buildings, built in 1782 on the site of what was then the Poor House; by Thomas Baldwin the city architect, and now the branch premises of various banks. Further down the street is the Octagon Chapel built in 1767 by Thomas Lightoler, whose skill as a carver and modeller is reflected in the plasterwork of the interior. Open to the public when not in use. Now if you walk towards Burton Street and then into Union Street you will return to Abbey Churchyard.

WALK 6.
Queen's Parade—Royal Crescent—Lansdown Crescent—Beckford's Tower

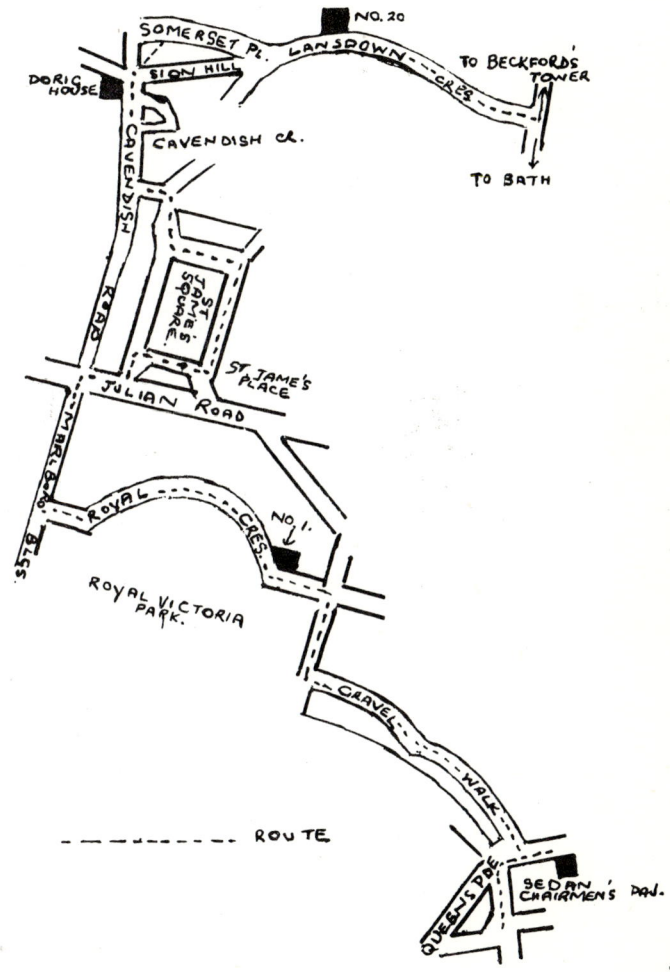

The Neo-Classical style in architecture was firmly established in Bath by John Wood the Younger in his design for the Royal Crescent. The squares and terraces of the Woods had given Bath the lead in Palladian building, and in creating the **Royal Crescent** it has been said that John Wood had in mind Bernini's colonnade surrounding the Piazza San Pietro in Rome. The "Bath Chronicle" for Thursday May 21st 1767 records that, "on Tuesday last the foundation stone was laid of the first house of the intended new building above the Circus called the Royal Crescent". This referred to No. 1 built for Thomas Brock the architect's father-in-law, and whose name is commemorated in nearby Brock Street. No. 1 has had many residents, at one time the Princesse de Lamballe, friend of Marie Antoinette, the ill-fated consort of Louis XVI, lived here in 1787. Then in 1796 the "Grand Old Duke of York who had ten thousand men", finding the mineral waters helped to restore his health, lived here for a while, but now, in the most distinguished corner house in Bath, the Bath Preservation Trust has its headquarters. The house was given to the Trust by Major Cayzer together with funds to restore it. The restoration has now been completed and the interior contains an interesting collection of authentic Georgian furniture and paintings. During the spring and summer the house is open to the public.

This walk takes in the Crescent and so on this occasion the starting point is **Queen's Parade** in the north west corner of Queen Square at the entrance to the Royal Victoria Park. Queen's Parade is a pleasant terrace built by John Wood II in 1769, it was at one time the intended site for the upper assembly rooms, but disagreement among the shareholders led to the project being turned down. At No. 10 lived Mrs. Maria Fitzherbert, morganatic wife of George IV. Now walk into Queen's Parade Place, and on the right hand side you will see two small pavilions (Wood 1730), both carefully restored. Here the Sedan chairmen would wait to be hired and the proceedings were succinctly recounted by an 18th century gentleman to a friend in Venice: "We are carried to these places in Sedan chairs which are very cheap, a guinea a week or a shilling per hour, and your chairmen serves you as porters as your gondoliers do in Venice".

Sedan Chairmen's Pavilions.

On the opposite side steps lead into Gravel Walk and a short walk will give you the first glimpse of Royal Crescent, a truly impressive sight. At No. 4 lived Christopher Anstey, author of "The New Bath Guide". 1771 saw the Linley family, having moved from Orchard Street, settled at No. 11, or were they? For on a March evening in 1772 the family were engaged at a concert, but not Elizabeth; she had pleaded illness, but during the evening a carriage pulled up outside No. 11 into which Elizabeth stepped, making the first scene of her elopement with Richard Sheridan. No. 17 was the home for a considerable time of Sir Isaac Pitman.

At the far end of the Crescent turn right into Marlborough Buildings and walk to Julian Road. To the right of Cavendish Road opposite is the entrance to St. James' Square commenced in 1790 to plans submitted by John Palmer. The land at one time consisted of orchards and gardens, one plot being in the possession of Christopher Anstey who received his notice to quit with no good favour and wrote the following against the planners who had taken his gardens from him:—

"Ye men of Bath, who stately mansions rear,
To wait for tenants from the de'il knows where,
Would you pursue a plan which cannot fail,
Erect a madhouse, and enlarge your jail."

Leading off the south east corner is St. James' Street; note the pedimental archway entrance leading to St. James' Place, one of those out-of-the-way courts which add so much to the character of Bath. Further along at No. 35 Charles Dickens would stay on his many visits to the City. From the far end of the Square it is but a few steps along to Park Place and into Cavendish Road: on your right is the fine terrace of Cavendish Place (1808) and further up the slope is **Cavendish Crescent** (1817). This is where the classical architecture of the Woods and Palmer give way to the more austere Regency style of John Pinch. Walk now to where Sion Hill joins the Cavendish Road, and to the Doric House on the corner, built possibly around 1810 by Joseph Gandy for the painter Thomas Barker (1769–1847). Barker came to Bath in 1782 from Wales under the patronage of Charles Spackman, a wealthy coachbuilder, studied in Italy and returned to England in 1793, inspired. The reason for building this house was to allow Barker to install his picture gallery, and to paint the enormous fresco "Massacre of Scio". The interior also includes a delicate wrought iron balustrade, and some fine moulded plasterwork. Walk across to the steps opposite and climb the footpath into Somerset Place (Eveleigh 1793) which forms the western wing of the serpentine curve created by Lansdown Crescent. Note the attractive centre piece of two houses supporting a broken pediment decorated with festoons and pendants.

Move along next to **Lansdown Crescent,** built from designs by John Palmer for Charles Spackman in 1789 and from whom the crescent received one of its former names, Spackman's Buildings. At No. 20 lived Bath's great eccentric, William Beckford, son of a former Lord Mayor of London, and at 24 M.P. for Wells. He wrote "Vathek", an eastern tale in French,

Lansdown Crescent.

at a single sitting, but tiring of politics he began building in 1796 the magnificient mansion of Fonthill in Wiltshire which he set about furnishing with considerable taste and luxury. A change in his fortunes compelled him to sell these estates and in 1822 he retired to Bath with his devoted servant, the dwarf Perro. Beckford joined two houses with a bridge, leased a large area of land at the rear of both houses and proceeded to transform the whole into a series of elaborate plantations. At the highest point of his garden and in order that he might see across to Fonthill, Beckford built in 1825 his 154 foot high folly. Apparently, Henry Goodridge, the architect employed by this unusual man, found inspiration in designing the Tower from the Lysicrates Monument in Athens. Both employer and architect are buried in the adjoining cemetery.

The Tower is open to the public and by walking to the end of

Royal Crescent.

the Crescent to where it joins the Lansdown Road, and then turning left, a gradual climb through Bath's Victorian and Edwardian environs brings you to this hilltop landmark. Although the building is not in Bath it is essentially of it, and in fact until its recent purchase belonged to the parishioners of Walcot, a gift from Beckford's daughter. Their rector a few years back harshly referred to it as a "pain in the neck", and was at a loss to know how to rid the parish of this unwanted burden. The Tower has been sympathetically restored by its new owner, Doctor Hilliard of Batheaston, and a visit would justify the slog from Bath. There is, of course, a bus which passes the entrance and which will return you to Bath.

WALK 7.
Abbey Green—Pierrepont Street—Pulteney Bridge—Sydney Place

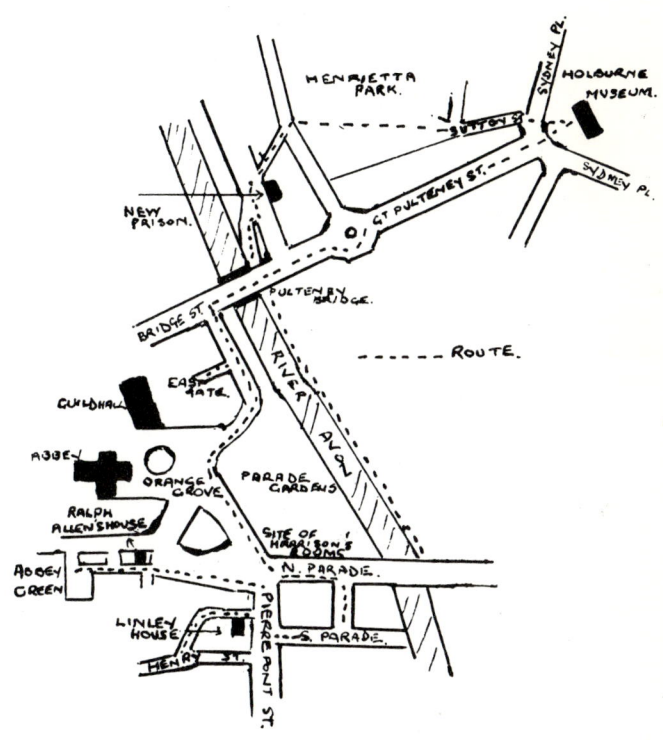

Abbey Green, a remnant of the former great monastic establishment of Bath: except perhaps for one small fragment, a hinge reputed to be part of the Abbey gateway, there is little to remind you of the extensive buildings. The gateway led to the orchards and meadows beyond the monastic precincts and the hinge can be seen set in the wall on the far side of Marks and Spencer's "historic" contribution to the City, St. Michael's Arch. Yet at the time of the suppression of the monasteries the monastic buildings were occupying nearly a quarter of the town. Henry VIII's ruthless commissioners appointed for its spoliation offered to sell the buildings for a derisory sum to the City, but the offer was refused and the Abbey fell on hard times, until a Matthew Colthurst purchased the now sadly dilapidated buildings. In 1560 what were now virtually ruins were presented to the City by Edmund Colthurst, Matthew's son, but it took another 40 years before any restoration took place, and that only accounted for the Abbey Church; for the rest, final decay.

Abbey Green makes a pleasant start to this walk, and has the best plane tree of any square in Bath. It has long been discovered that planes are the only trees which thoroughly enjoy a town atmosphere:–

"Green is the plane-tree in the square,
The other trees are brown,
They droop and pine for country air,
The plane-tree loves the town."

Amy Levy.

Have a look at the fine house on the corner of Abbey Street and York Street, and note the pedimental dormer windows and the excellent front door. Before entering Abbey Green, walk along towards the river, passing a row of shops to where the Society of Friends (Quakers) have their meeting house, which was built in 1819 by William Wilkins, the architect responsible for the National Gallery and the Gothic screen to King's College, Cambridge. Now locate an iron gateway between the meeting house and an antique shop, which open on to a quiet courtyard where the great Ralph Allen would sit in his large garden commanding fine views of Bathampton Down, and where later he built his whimsical eyecatcher Sham Castle. After Allens occupation of Prior Park, the gardens were encroached upon, and disappeared under successive building schemes leaving only this small courtyard and a figtree as a reminder. The garden front of Allen's Town House, built possibly in 1728, has been sympathetically restored, displaying the elaborate Palladianism of John Wood. Above the rusticated ground storey rises four engaged columns with Corinthian capitals which divide the front into three bays, the middle one being dominated by a fine arched window. It was from this house that Allen carried on his business as Postmaster for Bath.

The ghost of Ralph Allen must have fallen about with laughter at the G.P.O.'s two tiered postal service, for in 1720 this Cornish innkeeper's son offered the government £6000 a year for the right to run the country's provincial post. Allen pulled the country postal service out of the chaos created by letters being routed through London by introducing a six-days-a-week cross-country system and made an annual profit of £12,000, a large sum in the early 18th century.

On returning to Abbey Green enter **North Parade Passage**—formerly known as Lilliput Alley, why was it altered? Along on the left is one of the oldest houses in Bath, it was built for the Dukes of Kingston in the 15th century and later became famous as Sally Lunn's cake shop, a reminder of how Bath looked before the era of the Woods. A reminder too of Princess Anne's visit in 1692 accompanied by her husband George of Denmark and the over-zealous Lady Marlborough, a visit that caused a Royal storm and a reprimand of the Mayor by Queen Mary with whom the Princess had quarrelled.

Hard by is **North Parade Buildings,** originally called Gallaway's Buildings, built between 1742 and 1745, possibly by the architect Thomas Jelly for an apothecary, William Gallaway. Here lived John Palmer who pioneered the first English mail coach. His father was the promoter of the new theatre in Old Orchard Street, but it was the son who first secured in Bath the first Theatre Royal outside London and later another at Bristol, and because travelling between the two theatres created a major headache he was successful in getting the Bristol, Bath to London road improved followed in 1784 by the introduction of the first mail coach to London.

Cross the space in front of the Fernley Hotel to the entrance of **Pierrepont Street** and walk to St. James's Portico. On the other side at No. 2 would come the Rev. Edmund Nelson and family each winter for a month or so to escape the cold winds of Norfolk, and Horatio, as a junior naval officer, would stay here after a tour of duty abroad. Passing under the Portico you enter **Pierrepont Place:** at Linley House, now the offices of the Festival Society, lived the musical family of Linley from 1767 to 1771. Thomas Linley was a composer of note later to become musical director of the Drury Lane Theatre, Tom, his son, a violinist of considerable merit and a great friend of Mozart, and daughter Elizabeth (The Fair Maid of Bath) a brilliant singer who at the age of 18 became the wife of Richard Sheridan. Another member of this versatile household was a servant named Emma Hart who later became Lady Hamilton and mistress of Lord Nelson. Considerable restoration has been undertaken in this little corner, and in Old Orchard Street around the corner is the old Theatre Royal mentioned earlier, and now a Masonic Hall.

You have now come to **Henry Street,** over on your right is the hideous shopping precinct development which swallowed up Southgate Street, an area of small nondescript late Georgian houses, and only recently completed, but turn left towards Pierrepont Street and cross to South Parade. North and South Parades were part of Wood's grandiose scheme for developing the Abbey Orchard site; Wood had a wild idea of creating "The Royal Forum of Bath"; it met serious opposition and left only the two Parades to show for Wood's original enthusiasm. You have now arrived at the entrance of Duke Street, now a quiet pedestrian precinct amid pedimented Georgian houses, a short walk leads into North Parade where at No. 9 William Wordsworth lodged in 1841. and No. 11 saw the occupation of Oliver Goldsmith in 1771.

Now cross to the balustrade surrounding **Parade Gardens,** originally known as Harrison's Walks and which was for many years a favoured spot for fashionable society. On the corner Thomas Harrison in 1708 built Bath's original Assembly Rooms, persuaded by that arbiter of fashion Beau Nash. After

Pulteney Bridge.

an initial success its popularity declined, partly destroyed by fire it was later rebuilt to house the Royal Literary Institution and finally demolished in 1933. **The Grand Parade** opens into Orange Grove, renamed to commemorate the visit of the Prince of Orange in 1734 who confessed to having benefited from the waters, gave Nash a gold snuffbox and in return Nash caused the obelisk to be erected.

You have now arrived at that point of Grand Parade where you can look down into the River Avon and at Robert Adam's **Pulteney Bridge** (1769–74). Aesthetically much harm has been done to this beautiful bridge, but looking from where you are standing it still presents a delightful study of Palladian architecture. The Bathwick estates on the east side of the river had been brought to William Johnstone by his marriage to Frances Pulteney, which caused him to add his wife's name to his own.

The now William Johnstone Pulteney proposed to develop his property as a garden city estate for persons of quality. Pulteney's friend Robert Adam prepared the pilot scheme, but because of local rivalry and prohibitive costs his plans were abandoned. The bridge was completed and the purchase by Pulteney of the ruined church of St. Mary's Northgate gave access to the bridge (Bridge Street) from the High Street to the future Great Pulteney Street (1788).

Before crossing the bridge cross the road to the entrance of Boat Stall Lane (sometimes referred to as Newmarket Row) alongside the Grove Hotel. A few yards ahead is Bath's only remaining gateway—East Gate—for pedestrian use only, and which gave access to the ferry crossing to Bathwick.

Return to the bridge and cross to **Argyle Street,** on the north side is the Congregational Chapel, incongruous in every detail, yet interesting as an example of the effect which simple largeness of detail can produce. The evangelist William Jay, the finest pulpit orator of his time, preached here for 62 years ending with his death in 1854. One can say of him that no one is more zealous for a cause than the convert. Beyond Argyle Street is Laura Place where a new fountain, pedestrian in character, was erected in 1977 and once more as in the 18th century dominates the entrance to Great Pulteney Street. No. 15 Johnstone Street on the south side of Laura Place was the residence for a short time of William Pitt, son of the Earl of Chatham; whilst here he received the bitter news of the allied defeat by Napoleon at Austerlitz (1805).

Laura Place now opens into **Great Pulteney Street,** perhaps the most impressive street in Bath. It was built to designs submitted by Thomas Baldwin whose plans for transforming Bathwick into a townscape of beautiful squares and terraces came to an abrupt halt in 1793 when Baldwin was declared bankrupt, having already been dismissed earlier as City Architect.

The Holburne of Menstrie Museum (open to the public) makes an impressive backdrop to Great Pulteney Street which now merges into the hexagon formed by Sydney Place and Beckford Road. The Museum was originally built as the Sydney Hotel to the designs of Harcourt Masters in 1796 to serve the

Vauxhall pleasure gardens at the rear. The gardens became so popular that the hotel constructed a public house in the basement calling it the Sydney Tap, but decline set in when public taste changed, and the buildings were in a semi-derelict condition when in 1915 the trustees of Sir Thomas Holburne purchased them to house his Fine Art Collection.

At No. 103 **Sydney Place** the Duke of Clarence, later William IV, lived for a short while and at No. 4 Jane Austen lived from 1801 to 1805. Walk past No. 4 to Sutton Street and follow this street to where it leads into Henrietta Park, named after Pulteney's daughter Henrietta Laura, who followed in her father's footsteps in developing Bathwick. Walk across the park to where Henrietta Street joins Henrietta Road, locate a passageway adjoining a primary school and walk along to Grove Street, a rather shabby little street but improved recently with the restoration of the New Prison (1772 Atwood)—so called to distinguish it from the Old Prison housed in the tower of St. Mary's Northgate, purchased by William Pulteney, who also gave in exchange the land for the prison site in Grove Street. At the south end of Grove Street a lane forking to the right leads through an archway formed by Argyle Street giving access to a pleasant riverside walk back to North Parade.

WALK 8.
Bear Flat—Beechen Cliff—Lyncombe Hill—Prior Park—Widcombe

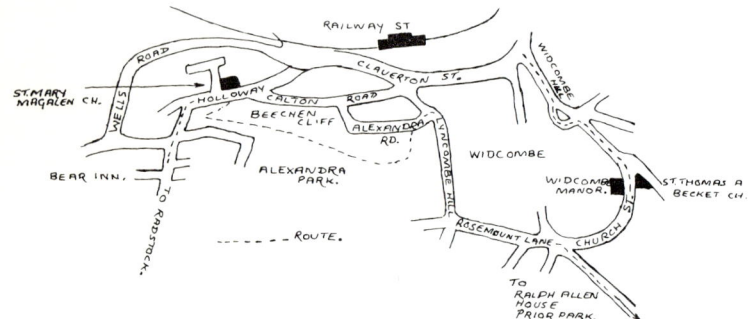

Very little has been told so far about Ralph Allen in these walks around Bath, and yet he was the mastermind behind Bath's 18th century rise to fame. His initial success came in the postal service, firstly by revealing as a result of a suspicious letter an intended Jacobite rising—a touchy subject in those days—thus securing for himself the postmastership of Bath, and secondly his success with the "cross country mails" mentioned in a previous walk. With his new found wealth he invested in the Combe Down stone quarries just about in time to make a second fortune. Allen tendered for the supply of Bath stone for the Greenwich Hospital (now the Royal Naval College), but the architects Colin Campbell, John James, and Nicholas Hawksmoor were not impressed and refused to use it. Allen was piqued and to show all and sundry the quality of bath stone built Prior Park. Work began in 1735 and finished in 1743, the architect being John Wood. Prior Park is an exquisite example of Neoclassical architecture, but on conversion to a boy's college in 1830 extensive alterations took place, depriving the buildings of much of Wood's original design.

Ralph Allen encouraged brilliant men of letters to his dinner table, including many leading statesmen of the day, in fact William Pitt owed his seat in Parliament as M.P. for Bath to Allen. The salon at Prior Park has been compared to Holland House in Kensington where under Lord Holland the house attained a splendour and beauty to become the intellectual centre not only for England, but for the world. This is regrettably a too ambitious comparison. Allen died in 1764 and he is buried with members of his family in the hillside churchyard of Claverton. He left to posterity a City of grace and dignity without equal.

This walk commencing from the **Bear Flat** includes a visit to Prior Park, so walk or take the bus to the top of the Wells Road, and from the Bear Inn walk back towards Holloway. This road was at one time the main approach from the south to Bath and followed the Roman Fosseway into the City, and as the name indicates it formed a well defined declivity under Beechen Cliff. Holloway of 140 years ago was vastly different in appearance from that seen today, it was so rugged and steep that the citizens of Bath and the packhorses took the more circuitous trackway to the north west of Holloway, and as the years passed this route developed into what we know today as the Wells Road.

Walk along the old flagstone pavement raised above the road and on your left you will soon reach St. Mary Magdalen Chapel. Built by Prior Cantlow in 1495, it was part of the ancient charity known as the Hospital of St. Mary Magdalen, annexed to the Bath Priory in the reign of Henry I. In Magdalen Road hard by is Magdalen House, the former home of the monks in medieval times who were sent from Bath to care for the lepers and the poor who stayed here before entering the City. Further along is Paradise House, built about 1740, all that remains of "a fair street as a suburb to the City", the historian Leland's words, for further down Holloway an improvement scheme has usurped the site of this historic entry into Bath.

Now retrace your footsteps to the far side of the road and to a sad looking horsetrough badly mauled by the ravages of time and neglect. There used to be a board on which there was a verse pleading for mercy for the cruelly treated horses which apparently hauled coal from the North Somerset coal mines to Bath. The trough was said to be erected at a spot where a horse was flogged to death by its master.

"A man of kindness to his beast is kind,
But brutal actions show a brutal mind,
Remember He who made thee made the brute,
He gave thee power of speech but made him mute,
He can't complain, but God's all seeing eye,
Beholds thy cruelty and hears his cry,
He was designed thy servant not thy drudge,
Remember his creator is thy judge."

Now for the climb to **Beechen Cliff;** the entrance to the steps is a few yards higher up. Once on top walk along to where there is a break in the trees which enshrouds this final escarpment of the Somerset Hills. You cannot fail to be impressed by the magnificent townscape of Bath before you, revealing a skyline of fine Georgian terraces, church spires, and dominating it all the centuries old Abbey Church, but below you the eye will not miss the modern excresence which development has created in the southern end of the City, and which stands out like a sore thumb. Continue walking along this footpath, passing Alexandra Park on your right, until you reach a steep flight of steps taking you down to Alexandra Road. On reaching the lower level turn right and walk to **Lyncombe Hill,** turn right again and climb to Rosemount Lane where several roads meet. Turn into Rosemount Lane which now falls away steeply to join Ralph Allen Drive at the bottom. At this point you can decide whether to continue into Church Street opposite or walk up Ralph Allen's Drive to **Prior Park.** Should you choose the latter you will not be disappointed for it is a pleasant walk, and before long the first entrance gates are reached. Ignore these and continue to the main gates of **Prior Park College.** Enter the college precincts by means of a wicket gate on the side of a lodge and follow the footpath carefully, remembering that the grounds are private to the steps fronting the main house. Wood originally provided for flights of steps down from the North Portico, but they were never built. However, in 1830 Bishop Baines, the founder of Prior Park College, commissioned

Goodridge to design the flight of steps you see now. The views down the valley towards Bath are truly magnificient.

The parkland originally belonged to the Priory of Bath before the dissolution and extended down towards the Avon. The little Palladian Bridge at the foot of the combe was built about 1755 over the fishponds, and is a copy of the bridge which spans the River Nadder at Wilton House. Before leaving do take a look inside the chapel which is alongside the footpath, it is mostly of the mid-19th century and does somehow conflict with the earlier Georgian buildings.

Thomas à Becket Church, Widcombe.

Now return to Ralph Allen's Drive and retrace your steps to the corner of Church Street and walk into Widcombe. Very soon you will see ahead **Widcombe Manor,** the Golden House of the author Horace Vachell who lived here for many years. In the early 18th century it belonged to Phillip Bennett, at one

Townscape of Bath from Prior Park.

time M.P. for Bath, who remodelled the house and refaced it with Bath stone in 1727. It is however uncertain who built the original house, possibly Inigo Jones. Opposite the Manor is the parish church of Thomas à Becket, built by William Birde, Prior of Bath, in 1502 on the site of a Norman Church. The churchyard was a favourite spot with Walter Landor who purchased here a plot for his own resting place, but dying at Florence he was buried there. Further along Church Street is Widcombe Lodge with so many literary associations with Henry and Sarah Fielding and where much of Fielding's "Tom Jones" was completed.

At the end of Church Street is Widcombe Crescent and Terrace built about 1805, the architect is uncertain, possibly Thomas Baldwin or Harcourt Masters. At No. 1 lived Sir James Brook, 1st Rajah of Sarawak. Widcombe Hill is the continuation of Church Street and walking down it brings you to Claverton Street and back to Bath.

WALK 9.
Kennet & Avon Canal Towpath—Bathampton—Dundas—Monkton Combe—Combe Down—Widcombe

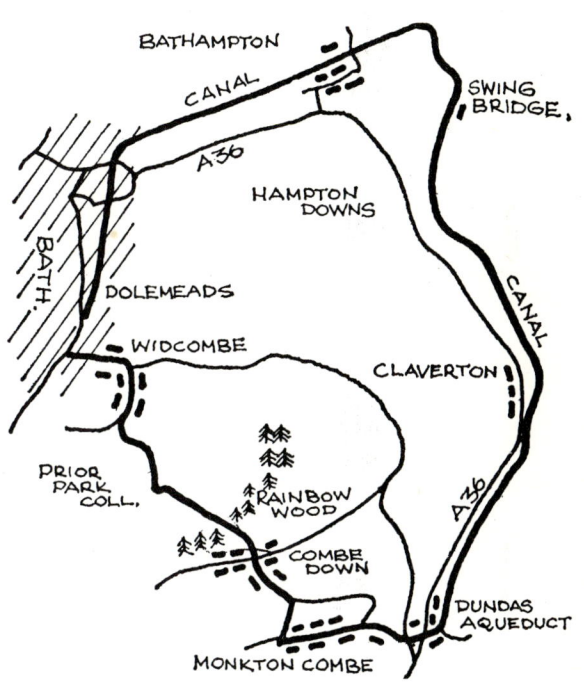

Nostalgia is a popular affliction. It is as though, defeated by the present, we take temporary refuge in the past.

This is partly why canals are being revived. Yet it's not just preservation for preservation's sake, but the restoration of derelict waterways to serve a useful purpose again by providing space with attractive surroundings in which people can spend their leisure time.

So my walk this time takes you along the towing path of the **Kennet and Avon Canal,** leaving it at the Dundas aqueduct to cross Claverton Down and then to slip down into Widcombe and so back to Bath.

It is a beautiful walk; once you have shaken yourself free of the Pulteney Road and entered the towpath at the bridge end of **St. Matthew's Place,** you're in the green and reedy world of the canal. While still in the heart of the city, you seem to plunge suddenly into the countryside.

A flight of seven locks—the Widcombe Flight—takes the canal uphill, and out of the centre of Bath; the first two, **Lower Lock** and **Chapel Lock** on the river side of the Pulteney Road Bridge, are now part of the highway improvement scheme.

But the remaining five, thanks to the enthusiasm of members of the Kennet and Avon Canal Trust, are in ship-shape order, and already well landscaped.

Bridge Lock No (9) is in the process of being restored by the highway authority. Further along is **Wash House Lock No (10),** and a cast-iron footbridge built by Stothert's in 1800. It's heartwarming to see the little wharves, long since abandoned, made into attractive backwaters.

The towpath crosses **Horseshoe Walk.** If you look to your left, you will notice hidden behind a hedge, the classical chimney of the flight pumping station, the centre of an early 19th century industrial storm.

Two more locks are passed, **Abbey View (No 11)** and **Pulteney (No 12),** and then another Stothert cast-iron footbridge which leads to Sydney Buildings.

Lock 13, the Top Lock, is next, and across on the other bank you will see the restored malthouse, recalling that the canal was used for transporting Somerset grain as well as Somerset coal; at a steady 2 mph it was slow, but reliable and cheap.

The Widcombe Flight, Kennet & Avon Canal.

How many of you plodding the towpath realise how much is owed to the enterprise of those early canal builders? Men like John Rennie, the chief engineer for the K and A, who performed impossible tasks on the land 200 years ago, tunnelling into hillsides, building aqueducts and complicated lock systems, and then having to compete with rising costs of construction in the uncertain year of 1793–4, a period of considerable financial crises resulting from the outbreak of the French Revolution.

You will by now have crossed the **George Street** bridge and be approaching the tunnel under **Cleveland House,** one-time headquarters of the canal company and former home of the Duke of Cleveland, the 18th century Lord of the Manor of Bathwick.

Before entering the tunnel you will have to cross to the other bank. Once you're through, continue along the cutting through **Sydney Gardens,** where the canal is spanned by some more of Stotherts' elegant footbridges.

The canal, already in financial difficulties, incurred more expense in having to pay the proprietors of Sydney Gardens 2,000 guineas for the right to take the canal through their property.

It is a pleasant walk through the gardens; after passing into the tunnel at the far end you emerge on the other side of the **Beckford Road Bridge,** following the towpath which is now just above the railway. Looking ahead you will see the lofty tower of St Saviour's church and, beyond, Little Solsbury Hill.

By the time you have reached **Meadow Farm Bridge,** known locally as "Suicide Bridge" because of the number of suicides that have occurred here, the environs of Bath have been left behind and you are now well into the countryside.

Soon the towpath turns into **Bathampton.** On the opposite bank there used to be a large granary with a wharf, and behind stood the stabling for the horses which pulled the horsebus from Bath to Bathampton. This has all disappeared, and a modelling clay factory occupies the site.

Pull off the towpath at the **George Inn** and visit the church of **St Nicholas.** It was largely rebuilt by Ralph Allen in 1754, and is currently in the throes of further improvements with the introduction of the Australia Chapel and Phillip Memorial.

Admiral Arthur Phillip, first governor of New South Wales and founder of Australia, together with his wife, is buried in the south aisle of the church.

The Chapel and Phillip Memorial was officially consecrated on January 26, 1975, the cost of construction being met by business houses in Australia.

Near neighbours in the churchyard are the graves of the ill-fated Elsie Luke, murdered on Hampton Down, and Viscount Du Barre, killed in a duel by his friend, Colonel Rice.

Returning to the towpath you will soon reach the **Swingbridge,** and if by now it is tea or coffee you need, then more than likely it could be served by Lady Knill.

Sir John inherited the title last year. Rather than the aloof dignity of the manorial mansion on the borders of Radnor and

Herefordshire, they prefer their humble lengthman's cottage and the watery world of the moorhen and the swan. They run a waterbus and offer refreshments at their canalside retreat.

Beyond the swingbridge the canal, railway, and river run close together into the **Limpley Stoke Valley.** Low wooded hills rise on either side; the towpath becomes a little more uneven, and the canal more reedy and overgrown.

Walking for two miles brings you to the **Dundas Aqueduct,** named after Charles Dundas, first chairman of the Kennet and Avon canal company, and **Dundas Wharf,** from where you take the uphill track to the **A36,** cross into the lane opposite and continue into **Monkton Combe** village.

Where the lane makes a sharp right hand turn near the church, locate the footpath which will take you up to **Shaft Road.**

On reaching the lane turn left and continue to **North Road,** where you cross into the woods opposite.

Follow the track to where it ends and then join the footpath bearing left across **Monument Field,** a name given locally because of a tower that once stood in the centre of the field, erected it is said by Bishop Warburton, son-in-law of Ralph Allen.

The pathway passes through **Rainbow Wood** and you leave by a kissing gate and follow the iron railings for about 100 yards to an upright pillar—possibly a disused gatepost.

From here bear left towards the boundary walls of **Prior Park.** The descent is quite steep, but do pause and look down the valley at the townscape of Bath. It is truly wonderful.

In the far corner you will find the stile. Continue to follow the footpath alongside a cottage garden to join a metalled trackway. Look back towards your right and you will see the Palladian bridge spanning the lake, which is a major feature of the landscaping of Prior Park.

A few yards further along the lane a footpath on your left leads to **Church Street,** and to the splendid early 18th century **Widcombe Manor.** Opposite is the late 15th century church of **St Thomas à Becket** and a little further along Church Street is **Widcombe Lodge,** where Henry and Sarah Fielding once lived.

Widcombe Hill joins Church Street, and from here you return to Bath.

WALK 10.
Bathampton—Bathford—Conkwell—Brassknocker Hill—Claverton Down

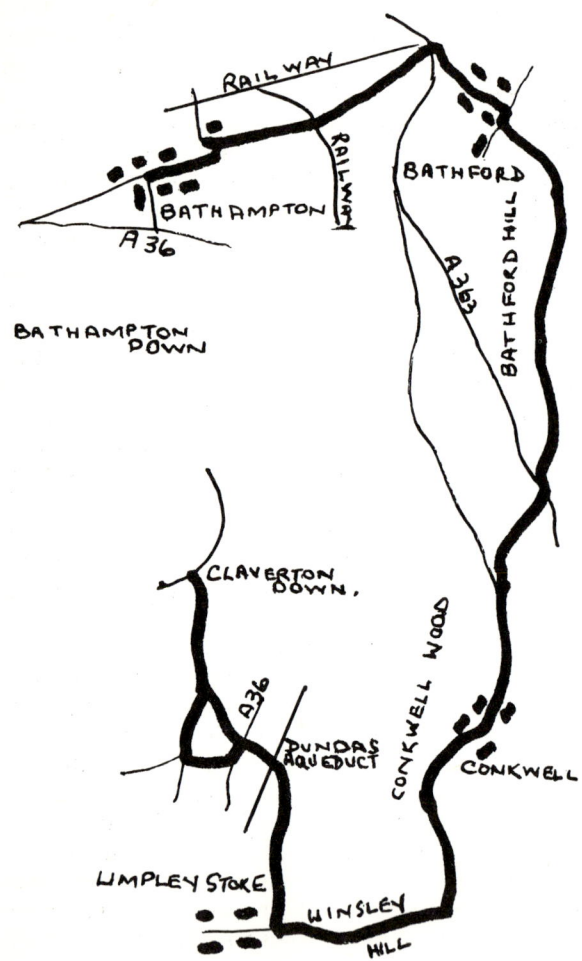

The River Avon makes an interesting waterscape at Bathampton as it makes a sudden turn south joining forces with the Kennet & Avon Canal to flow into the Limpley Stoke valley. On one side is the spur of Bathford Hill and Conkwell Woods, and on the other Bathampton and Claverton Downs. A noble scene enhanced by the graceful curving of the river as it meanders along the valley.

The countryside on the left bank is pleasantly rural, and on this walk you are given the opportunity of exploring the hill country between Bathford and Conkwell. Take the bus from the City Centre to **Bathampton** and alight at the High Street end of Down Lane. A walk along the High Street and across the canal bridge brings you to the little church of St. Nicholas. The churchyard is full of ancient tombs, and in one lies the Viscount du Barré, the favourite nephew of the notorious Madame du Barré, at one time the mistress of Louis XV of France. The Viscount met his death in a duel with his friend, the Count Rice, on Bathampton Down, why they quarrelled no one seems to know, but the body was brought to the George Inn, opposite, before burial in the churchyard. More important in the history of the church is its link with Australia. Many visitors from "down under" come to see where their founder lies, for Admiral Arthur Phillip, first governor of New South Wales, the man who led the first batch of settlers to Australia in 1788 has finally received the tribute he deserves. His grave has been lying in the chancel in relative obscurity for 160 years, but on January the 26th 1975 a new chapel was dedicated to his memory.

On leaving the church, turn left and enter the lane which leads past the schoolhouse and continue to where it comes to a halt at level crossing gates. Carefully cross the railway here and bear left, crossing two fields, to reach the railway embankment, and where the footpath continues over the river bridge and into the road leading into **Bathford.** Turn right and cross the bridge over a small stream (Box Brook) and enter the lane to the right of the "Crown Inn", and then climb to where it joins the village road near the church. Halt awhile here and enter the church through a Norman doorway into the spacious nave, take a look at the delicately carved pulpit, it is a real joy to see. To the left of the church, a narrow lane leads to Mountain Woods and within a short distance to the right, a footpath brings it on to Brown's Folly. The climb is quite steep, but you must pause, even at the risk of seeming to lag, to admire this scenic stretch along the Limpley Stoke valley.

Like so many follies up and down the country, the Tower was erected in 1840 by a Mr Wade Brown as an act of philanthropy in giving work to local craftsmen during a period of considerable depression which England suffered after the cessation of the Napoleonic Wars. A footpath leads along the ridge of Bathford Hill and within a mile of good walking the footpath falls away to make contact with the Bradford-on-Avon road (A363). On reaching the road, turn left and walk for about 100 yards or so along the main road to a bridge where, on the right, you will find a stile and the continuation of the footpath over Warleigh Hill giving, once more, views along the valley. A short walk brings you to the Bathford to Conkwell lane where you turn left along the "Sally in Woods" lane for Conkwell.

This was quarrying country at one time and you may notice how the hillside has been gouged away in places to produce the stone. Fortunately, nature has reclaimed her own, and now trees and vegetation have landscaped the ugly scars. **Conkwell** is a small hamlet and on reaching it, bear right to follow the lane along the ridge of Conkwell Woods, passing the entrance to Conkwell Grange, to bring you finally to Winsley Hill opposite the Winsley Chest Hospital.

Now turn right and walk down the hill to the bridge over the Kennet & Avon Canal, over on the right is the entrance to the towing path and a short, but pleasant, walk along the canalside leads to the Dundas Aqueduct. John Rennie, the canal engineer, took great pride in building this, and if you care to walk down the wooden steps on your left before crossing the aqueduct, you will obtain an excellent view of this masterpiece carrying the canal over the River Avon and the railway.

Having now crossed to the other side locate a steep footpath which runs at the rear of an old lengthmen's hut and which will take you past the grounds of Bassett House to the A36. Towards your right on the far side of the road there is a stile leading to a footpath up to **Brassknocker Hill,** or if you prefer, you can walk

Claverton Manor.

a short way along the main road, away from Bath, and enter a lane on your right, then at the next cross-roads, turn right and this will take you up Brassknocker Hill and to the bus stop at the top where the hill joins the Claverton Down Road to return you to Bath.

WALK 11.
Weston—Lansdown—Tadwick—Charlcombe

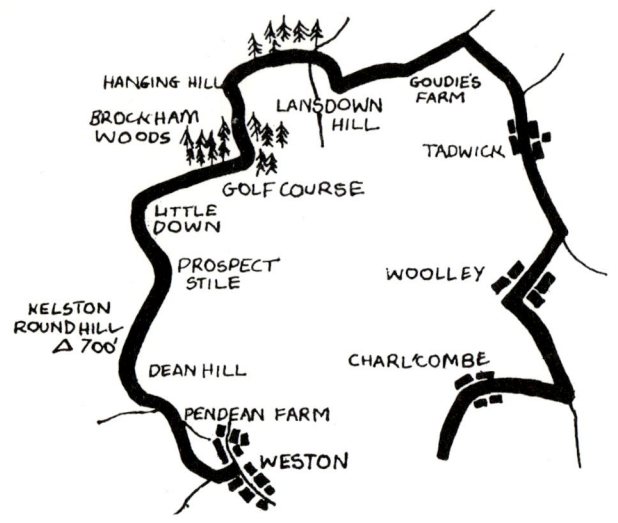

It is a great pity that the Cotswold Way has not been opened up as a national footpath.

It could then claim recognition from the Countryside Commission, financial assistance for the waymarking, signposting, and maintenance of the route, and of course the many other advantages now enjoyed by the users of The Ridgeway Path, Offa's Dyke Path, The Cornwall Coastal Path, and The Pennine Way, to name a few for which the Commission has a statutory responsibility.

The Cotswold Way Path runs for approximately 100 miles along the whole of the escarpment of the Cotswold Hills, starting from Chipping Campden in the heart of Gloucestershire, and finishing at Bath. To complete this marathon it would take well over a week's walking, but how rewarding. The object of my walks, however, is to give a route offering a day's walking, and pleasure in the countryside around or near to Bath, but which may include part of a national pathway easily accessible by bus or car. So on this walk I have taken part of The Cotswold Way where it enters Bath only walking in the opposite direction starting at Weston.

Walk or take a bus to **Weston,** and alight at Anchor Road, and continue into Penn Hill Road. At the far end of playing fields at the right hand of the road you will find a signpost indicating the Cotswold Way. Follow the footpath indicated and cross the stile on the left, climbing the hill ahead to the stile at the summit. You are now on the 400ft contour, and ahead is the OS Trig pillar. Below lies Weston village caught up in the tide of Bath's urban sprawl, and beyond, silhouetted against the skyline, is Beckford's Italian Campanile.

William Beckford left the ruins of his Fonthill folly a broken man. Fabulous were the riches of his inheritance, but they were lost in his pursuit of scholarship and art and not in dissipation as many would believe. He came to Bath and built his tower to enable him to see his former estates in Wiltshire. He would sit up here night after night with a candle poring over old books, a figure of amazing contrasts.

From Penn Hill the path descends slightly to join a lane at Pendean Farm. The route here is well signposted, and so follow the rough track which lies straight ahead. The track rises for Dean Hill, and over on your left is Kelston Roundhill. A detour can be made here to the OS Trig pillar just above the 700ft contour where you will obtain outstanding views of the countryside sweeping up from the levels of the River Avon.

Returning to your original path, continue the long climb up the other half of the saddleback, cross the lane to North Stoke (Via Julia) and on to Prospect Stile, probably Bath's best-known viewpoint. Here you can rest, and take in the panorama of the Avon winding and shining on its way through mile after mile of rolling pastureland, cupped by little hills, with the Welsh hills on the skyline.

From Prospect Stile the path leads to the left along the 700ft contour towards Little Down, an ancient hill fort, and away from the racecourse. Skirting Little Down, the path continues to the edge of Brockham Woods with the golf course on your right. When you come to the end of the woods, cross the golf course ahead to a track which brings the golf course, and Brockham Woods on to your left, and a large copse to your right. The track runs alongside a stone wall and soon crosses a newly-metalled track which leads to the left, across the golf course and to Brockham House. The track which you have been following comes to a clearing giving views of the Severn Valley. A few yards ahead you will see a gate bearing this portentous notice 'Keep within 10ft of wall and close the gate. Offenders automatically prosecuted'. With this welcome, go through the gate and follow the path skirting Hanging Hill to your left.

Ahead you will notice a radio mast. Follow the path to where

Sir Bevil Grenville's Monument, Lansdown.

it swings to the right towards this landmark, and where it eventually joins a track running alongside Beach Wood, and it will bring you to the main road leading to Bath.

This is **Lansdown,** the site of the Civil War battle fought here on a July day in 1643. When you reach the main road, turn right for 100 yards and then follow the signpost on your left pointing to the battle ground. You will reach a bulky stone monument, surmounted by a griffin which is approximately the spot where Sir Bevil Grenville fell mortally wounded leading his Cornish pikemen against the Parliamentary forces.

"Where shall the next fam'd Grenville's ashes stand?
The grandsire fills the seas, and thou the land."

The battle ground differs today practically not at all. Over towards the road the ridges and mounds leave little doubt they are of artificial formation, for it was here the Parliamentary troops threw up their earthworks, and entrenched their cannon. From here the path veers southwards through a field to a gate where you join a rough track going east with fine views of the Cotswold escarpment as it falls away to the Avon valley. The track descends slightly and is now enclosed by field walls on either side. You will come to a gate across the pathway, which on the other side starts to narrow. At this spot on your left is a signpost. Enter a field here and your way now leads down a steep slope to a stream and footbridge. As you approach you will see on your right Goudie's Farm. I was told by a lady from nearby Tadwick that the wounded Grenville was brought to this farm and that he died here, which would conflict with the accepted version that his followers brought him to Cold Ashton Manor and that he died there.

Once over the stream you part company with the Cotswold Way, which continues up the valley to Hill Farm. You will now come to Hall Lane, and the footpath that climbs up to Torneyscourt Farm and on into **Tadwick,** a delightful hamlet of stone cottages and dry stone walls. Follow the narrow lane south through the village, and very soon you will start going downhill into the combe of Langridge. However, ignore the lane on the right, and continue to climb the opposite hillside until, on reaching the Woolley signpost, you turn right and

Beckford's Tower.

follow the road over the stream for the village.

At the end of a lane with nicely-restored cottages on either side is John Wood the Younger's splendid little Georgian church, which 'Elizabeth Parker, lady of the manor of Woolley did order to be builded at her own charge' in 1761. The way back to Bath is to continue along Woolley Lane passing on your left Twinfield Farm to a T junction where you turn right for **Charlcombe**. Visit the church here, it shows its Norman beginnings, but it is interesting as the scene of the marriage of Henry Fielding, the novelist, to Charlotte Craddock in 1734. Sarah Fielding was buried here in 1768.

From here it is but a three-quarters of a mile walk along Richmond Road to St Stephen's church and into the Lansdown Road bringing you to Bath.